L. PORTNOFF

MINIATURE-FANTASIAS
for Violin and Piano

(For the cultivation of musical feeling and appreciation, and the development of tone and bowing technic)

No. 1. RUSSIAN FANTASIA No. 1, A MINOR
(I. Pos. or I.-III. Pos.)

No. 2. RUSSIAN FANTASIA No. 2, D MINOR (I.-III. Pos.)

No. 3. RUSSIAN FANTASIA No. 3, A MINOR
(I. Pos. or I.-III. Pos.)

No. 4. RUSSIAN FANTASIA No. 4, E MINOR
(I. Pos. or I.-III. Pos.)

BOSWORTH

Russische Fantasie № 1
Russian Fantasia № 1   Fantaisie russe № 1

Violino

Leo Portnoff

*)Der Fingersatz der 3. Lage (über den Noten) ist für mehr fortgeschrittene Spieler. | *) The fingering in the 3rd position (on the top of tne notes) is for more advanced pupils. | *)Le doigté de la 3e position, au dessus des notes, est pour élèves plus avancés.

Russische Fantasie № 1

Russian Fantasia № 1   Fantaisie russe № 1

Leo Portnoff

*)Der Fingersatz der 3.Lage (über den Noten) ist für mehr fortgeschrittene Spieler.

*) The fingering in the 3rd position (on the top of the notes)is for more advanced pupils.

*)Le doigté de la 3e position, au dessus des notes, est pour élèves plus avancés.

Largemento

B. & Co. 18722

Allegretto

Allegro

B. & Co. 18722

Violino

Printed and bound in Great Britain by
Caligraving Limited Thetford Norfolk

EASY CONCERTOS AND CONCERTINOS

VIOLIN & PIANO

Beer, L. J.	Op. 47.	CONCERTINO in E min.	(1st position)
Beer, L. J.	Op. 81.	CONCERTINO in D min.	(1st position)
Coerne, L. A.	Op. 63.	CONCERTINO in D maj.	(1st and 3rd position)
Drdla, F.	Op. 225.	CONCERTINO in A min.	(1st — 7th position)
Essek, P.	Op. 4.	CONCERTINO in G maj.	(1st position)
Have, W. Ten.	Op. 30.	CONCERTO in D	(Advanced)
Küchler, F.	Op. 11.	CONCERTINO in G maj.	(1st position)
Küchler, F.	Op. 12.	CONCERTINO in D maj.	(1st — 3rd position)
Küchler, F.	Op. 15.	CONCERTINO in D maj.	(1st and 3rd position)
Millies, H.		CONCERTINO in D maj. in the style of Mozart	(1st position)
Millies, H.		CONCERTO in D maj. in the style of Haydn	(1st — 7th position)
Mistowski, A.		CONCERTINO in A min.	(3rd and 5th position)
Mokry, J.		CONCERTINO in G maj.	(1st position)
Mozart, W. A.		CONCERTO No. 1 in G maj.	(1st position)
Muscat, H.	Op. 11.	CONCERTINO in D	(1st position)
Portnoff, L.	Op. 13.	CONCERTINO in E min.	(1st position)
Portnoff, L.	Op. 14.	CONCERTINO in A min.	(1st — 3rd position)
Rieding, O.	Op. 7.	CONCERTO in E min.	(1st — 7th position)
Rieding, O.	Op. 21.	CONCERTINO in A min.	(1st and 3rd position)
Rieding, O.	Op. 24.	CONCERTINO in G maj.	(1st, 3rd and 5th position)
Rieding, O.	Op. 25.	CONCERTINO in D maj.	(1st, 3rd and 5th position)
Rieding, O.	Op. 34.	CONCERTO in G maj.	(1st position)
Rieding, O.	Op. 35.	CONCERTO in B min.	(1st position)
Rieding, O.	Op. 36.	CONCERTO in D maj.	(1st position)
Seitz, F.	Op. 7.	CONCERTO in D	(3rd and 5th position)
Seitz, F.	Op. 12.	CONCERTO in G min.	(1st and 3rd position)
Seitz, F.	Op. 13.	CONCERTO in G	(1st position)
Seitz, F.	Op. 15.	CONCERTO in D	(3rd and 5th position)
Seitz, F.	Op. 22.	CONCERTO in D	(1st position)
Sitt, H.	Op. 70.	CONCERTINO in A min.	(1st — 5th position)

VIOLA & PIANO

Beer, L. J.	Op. 47.	CONCERTINO in E min.	(1st — 3rd position)
Beer, L. J.	Op. 81.	CONCERTINO in D min.	(1st — 3rd position)
Küchler, F.	Op. 11.	CONCERTINO in G maj.	(1st — 3rd position)
Mokry, J.		CONCERTINO in G maj.	(1st — 3rd position)
Rieding, O.	Op. 35.	CONCERTO in B min.	(1st — 3rd position)
Rieding, O.	Op. 36.	CONCERTO in D maj.	(1st — 3rd position)

'CELLO & PIANO

Beer, L. J.	Op. 47.	CONCERTINO in E min.	(1st — 7th position)
Beer, L. J.	Op. 81.	CONCERTINO in D min.	(1st — 7th position)
Küchler, F.	Op. 11.	CONCERTINO in G maj.	(1st — 7th position)
Mokry, J.		CONCERTINO in G maj.	(1st — 7th position)
Rieding, O.	Op. 35.	CONCERTO in B min.	(1st — 7th position)
Rieding, O.	Op. 36.	CONCERTO in D maj.	(1st — 7th position)
Seitz, F.	Op. 22.	CONCERTO in D	(1st — 7th position)

BOSWORTH

ISBN 978-1-78038-709-3

Order No: BOE004565

DISTRIBUTED BY
HAL LEONARD

14025890   8 84088 48702 7